Numbers

_____

Written by Stephen Barnett
Illustrated by Rosie Brooks

Contents

About this book

Here numbers are used to widen the scope of learning to read. Repetition of the numbers along with the colourful and interesting pictures of numbers help to associate meaning with the words the reader is learning.

Numbers

One

Two

Three

Here are three numbers.

There is one cat.

Here are
two kids.

I can see one boy.

I can see one girl.

Three birds are
on
one tree.

The cat has one kitten.

The kids
have two
ice creams.

The kids look at the birds.

Two kids, one cat and one kitten

The kitten is looking at the birds.

The birds fly away.

New words

are	I
away	ice cream
bird	kitten
boy	look
can	number
kids	one
fly	three
girl	two
have	

What did you learn?

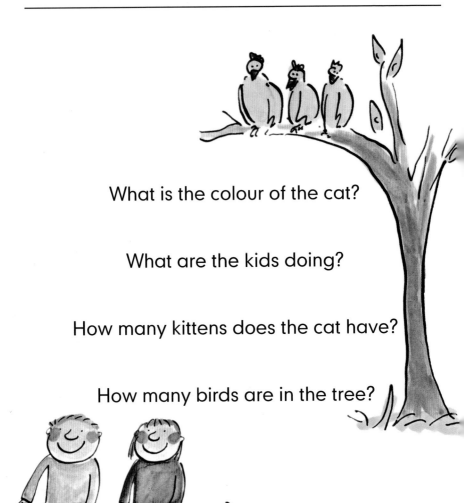

What is the colour of the cat?

What are the kids doing?

How many kittens does the cat have?

How many birds are in the tree?